THIS BOOK BELONGS TO:

_____

IF FOUND, PLEASE RETURN TO:

```
┌─────────────────────────────────┐
│                                 │
│   _____ │
│                                 │
│   _____ │
│                                 │
│   _____ │
│                                 │
└─────────────────────────────────┘
```

This book is dedicated to you.
Yes, you!
The person holding this journal in your hands.

Because you have something inside you—something strong,
something full of fire.
And when you believe in yourself, you become unstoppable.

I know, because I've been there. I've run, trained, doubted, tried again.
Stood on some of the biggest stages in the world and won medals.

And I want to help you find your version of unstoppable.
Not just in sport—but in anything that lights you up.

So let's get started. This is your space now. Let's make you
Unstoppable.

Text copyright © 2025 by Sasha Gollish / Yellow Running Shoes

Strong Girl Publishing | StrongGirlPublishing.com
First edition, 2025
ISBN 978-1-998743-04-9

Welcome to **Unstoppable!**

This journal is all about helping you train your brain, just like you train your body.

It's here to help you stay focused, confident, and resilient—whether you're heading to practice, trying something new, or getting ready for your biggest game of the season.

You don't have to write a lot. Just one minute before and one minute after practice or a competition can make a huge difference.

In here, you'll find:
- A space to get to know yourself as an athlete
- Tips for packing like a pro
- One-minute reflections before and after each practice
- Special tools to help you get game-day ready

It's not about being perfect.
It's about showing up.
Trying.
Learning.
Getting stronger every day—inside and out.

Because when you learn how to check in with your thoughts, notice your patterns, and stay grounded in your goals, you're building the tools that help you have your best day. And then another. And another.

Use it how it works best for you.
And remember: You're not just a player.
You're a whole person. **And you are unstoppable**.

HOW TO USE THIS BOOK

Unstoppable is your very own Mental Performance Journal. You might've heard pro athletes talk about things like:

- Mental toughness
- Resilience
- Focus
- Flow
- Confidence

Those are all part of something called mental performance, and that's what this journal is all about. It's not about being perfect. It's about learning to think like an athlete, so you can:

- Handle pressure better
- Stay focused during training and competition
- Bounce back when things don't go your way
- Believe in yourself—even when it's hard

Step 1: Know Yourself
Before you even get to the practice or game stuff, we start with a few short pages about you:

- What sport(s) you play
- What you're good at
- What you want to improve

Step 2: Use It Before and After Practice
Each time you train, take 1 minute before and 1 minute after to check in.

Before Practice:

- What are you excited for?
- What are you working on?
- What's making you nervous?

After Practice:
- What went well?
- What would you do differently next time?
- One word to describe how you feel, plus an emoji or a number to evaluate overall how practice was

That's it. You don't need to write a novel. This is your safe space to just be honest with yourself.

Step 3: Competition Days
Competition day = Game on.
Whether it's a race, match, meet, or tournament—you're getting ready to show what you've been working on.

This part of the journal helps you get organized and stay calm so you can focus, trust yourself, and compete with confidence.

On the competition pages, you'll check in on things like:
- What's the event? (Name + where it is)
- What's the weather? (Because rain, heat, and snow change how you prep!)
- What do I need to pack? (Uniform, gear, snacks, extras—no more missing socks!)
- What should I eat, and when? (So your body has energy to go!)
- How can I rest and recover? (Sleep = superpower.)

You'll also set a competition mantra—a short, powerful phrase to keep you focused. Something like:
- "I've got this."
- "Fast. Calm. Strong."
- "Eyes up. Heart open."
- **"I'm unstoppable."**

You can repeat your mantra before your race or game—or even write it on your hand.

This section helps you show up ready—physically and mentally—so that when the moment comes, you're not just hoping it'll go well... you're ready to make it your best day.

You might be reading this and asking <u>why</u>?

Why This Helps - Writing things down helps you:
- Focus better
- Train smarter
- Shake off the nerves
- Understand what makes you confident and resilient
- See how much you're growing

Even the pros do this—because your mindset is just as important as your muscles.

Bottom Line: This book is here to help you believe in yourself, one page at a time. Because the secret to being unstoppablel is learning how to show up—even on the hard days—and keep going.

I believe you already know what you need to make you unstoppable. You just need to learn how to tap into it.

You ready? Let's go.

Sasha

UNSTOPPABLE

**Step 1:
Know
Yourself**

STEP 1: KNOW YOURSELF

Who are you <u>right now</u>?

This section is a check-in with you as you are at this moment in time.
Not who you think you're supposed to be.
Not who others want you to be.
Just... you.

There are no right or wrong answers here.
This is your space to explore:
- What lights you up
- What makes you shut down
- What helps you show up and shine out

You'll come back to this later in the season, or in a few months, maybe even in a few days, and some things might have changed. That's normal. That's growth.

So grab a pen, pencil, your favourite colour marker, get honest and let's start with the most important part of sport: you.

LET'S START WITH THE BASICS

What sport or sports do you play?

_____

_____

What position(s) or event(s) do you compete in?

_____

_____

What is your favourite part of training or competing?

_____

_____

_____

What is the hardest part of training or competing?

_____

_____

_____

What are three words you'd use to describe yourself as an athlete?

_____

_____

_____

Draw your sport story so far—your jersey, your medal, your team, your gear, your favourite moment, or even just a feeling.

(There's no wrong way to do this. Draw whatever comes to mind when you think of yourself in sport.)

WHERE DO I FEEL MY SPORT SELF?

Instructions: Use this figure to show what you feel in your body before, during, or after a practice or game.

- Where do you feel excited?
- Where do you feel pressure or nerves?
- Where do you feel strong?

Some ideas to get you started:

for energy

for strength

for overthinking

for nervousness

for focus

(p.s. head to Instagram and tag @yellow_running_shoes and @stronggirlpublishing to share with us what other emojis and emotions we should add.)

JUST A FEW MORE QUESTIONS...

I feel most like me when I'm...

_____

_____

_____

A time I felt really proud of myself in sport was...

_____

_____

_____

A time I felt frustrated or unsure was...

_____

_____

_____

One thing that helps me feel brave...

_____

_____

_____

One thing I admire about my favourite athlete is ...

_____

_____

_____

JUST A FEW MORE QUESTIONS...

I show up best when....

_____

_____

_____

_____

_____

_____

I shut down when ...

_____

_____

_____

_____

_____

_____

If you want to revisit this use a blank sheet of paper and go through the
steps again or head over to StrongGirlPublishing.com/unstoppable

UNSTOPPABLE

Step 2:
Practice
Sessions

PACKING FOR PRACTICE

Being unstoppable starts before you even hit the pitch, pool, track, or court. Packing your bag the right way helps you feel ready, focused, and confident.

This is to help you remember what you need—and avoid those "oops I forgot my socks" kind of days.

Not all weather is created equally. We tried to think of some weather you might regularly see, plus a blank one for weather we have not thought of! You can always come back to add forgotten items. And there are additional 'Packing for Practice' sheets at strongirlpublishing.com/unstoppable.

In fact, take some time here and jot down a few notes about any packing issues you've had in the past. What have you forgotten often? Is there any piece of gear you wish you always had in your bag? What's the wildest weather you've ever practiced in?

_____

_____

_____

_____

_____

_____

_____

_____

Once you're packed, share with us on Instagram and tag @yellow_running_shoes and @stronggirlpublishing what your practice-ready bag looks like!

🔥 HOT & ☀ SUNNY DAYS

Uniform: _____

_____

Equipment: _____

_____

For Warm-up: _____

_____

For After: _____

_____

Pre-practice snacks: _____

During-practice snacks: _____

Post-practice snacks: _____

☐ Sunscreen   ☐ Extra-large water bottle

My sport specific extras: _____

_____

_____

 RAINY DAYS

Uniform: _____

_____

_____

Equipment: _____

_____

For Warm-up: _____

_____

For After: _____

_____

Pre-practice snacks: _____

During-practice snacks: _____

Post-practice snacks: _____

☐ Rain Coat & Umbrella ☐ Plastic Bag

My sport specific extras: _____

_____

_____

❄ COLD & 🌬 WINDY DAYS

Uniform: _____

_____

_____

Equipment: _____

_____

For Warm-up: _____

_____

For After: _____

_____

Pre-practice snacks: _____

During-practice snacks: _____

Post-practice snacks: _____

☐ Extra Coat   ☐ Towel or Blanket

My sport specific extras: _____

_____

_____

OTHER WEATHER: _____

Uniform: _____
_____
_____

Equipment: _____
_____

For Warm-up: _____
_____

For After Practice: _____
_____

Pre-practice snacks: _____

During-practice snacks: _____

Post-practice snacks: _____

☐ _____ ☐ _____

My sport specific extras: _____
_____
_____

STEP 2: PRACTICE SESSIONS

Every practice is a chance to get stronger—physically, mentally, emotionally, socially, spiritually.

And one of the best ways to do this? Take just one minute before and one minute after to check in with yourself.

That's what this section is for.

Use it to:
- Set your focus before practice
- Notice what you're feeling
- Reflect on what went well (and what didn't)
- Keep track of how you're getting stronger

There's no pressure to write a lot. Just a few honest thoughts.

Remember: your mind is like a muscle too—and these pages are your mental reps.

Today's Date:_____

BEFORE PRACTICE

Today I am most excited about:

_____

_____

One thing I feel nervous or unsure about:

_____

_____

My focus today is:

_____

_____

My mindset heading into today's practice:

☐ Calm
☐ Focused
☐ Tired
☐ Pumped
☐ Nervous
☐ Something else: _____

If I had to rate my mood out of 10: _____

AFTER PRACTICE

One thing that went well:

_____

_____

One thing I would do differently next time:

_____

_____

Today I had the most fun ...

_____

_____

My mindset after today's practice:

☐ Confident
☐ Frustrated
☐ Proud
☐ Unfocused
☐ Strong
☐ Something else: _____

One word to describe today's practice:

_____

If I had to rate my mood out of 10: _____

Today's Date:_____

BEFORE PRACTICE

Today I am most excited about:

_____

_____

One thing I feel nervous or unsure about:

_____

_____

My focus today is:

_____

_____

My mindset heading into today's practice:

☐ Calm
☐ Focused
☐ Tired
☐ Pumped
☐ Nervous
☐ Something else: _____

If I had to rate my mood out of 10: _____

AFTER PRACTICE

One thing that went well:

_____

_____

One thing I would do differently next time:

_____

_____

Today I had the most fun ...

_____

_____

My mindset after today's practice:

☐ Confident
☐ Frustrated
☐ Proud
☐ Unfocused
☐ Strong
☐ Something else: _____

One word to describe today's practice:

_____

If I had to rate my mood out of 10: _____

Today's Date:_____

BEFORE PRACTICE

Today I am most excited about:

_____

_____

One thing I feel nervous or unsure about:

_____

_____

My focus today is:

_____

_____

My mindset heading into today's practice:

☐ Calm
☐ Focused
☐ Tired
☐ Pumped
☐ Nervous
☐ Something else: _____

If I had to rate my mood out of 10: _____

AFTER PRACTICE

One thing that went well:

_____

_____

One thing I would do differently next time:

_____

_____

Today I had the most fun ...

_____

_____

My mindset after today's practice:

☐ Confident
☐ Frustrated
☐ Proud
☐ Unfocused
☐ Strong
☐ Something else: _____

One word to describe today's practice:

_____

If I had to rate my mood out of 10: _____

Today's Date:_____

BEFORE PRACTICE

Today I am most excited about:

_____

_____

One thing I feel nervous or unsure about:

_____

_____

My focus today is:

_____

_____

My mindset heading into today's practice:

☐ Calm
☐ Focused
☐ Tired
☐ Pumped
☐ Nervous
☐ Something else: _____

If I had to rate my mood out of 10: _____

AFTER PRACTICE

One thing that went well:

_____

_____

One thing I would do differently next time:

_____

_____

Today I had the most fun ...

_____

_____

My mindset after today's practice:

- ☐ Confident
- ☐ Frustrated
- ☐ Proud
- ☐ Unfocused
- ☐ Strong
- ☐ Something else: _____

One word to describe today's practice:

_____

If I had to rate my mood out of 10: _____

Today's Date:_____

BEFORE PRACTICE

Today I am most excited about:

_____

_____

One thing I feel nervous or unsure about:

_____

_____

My focus today is:

_____

_____

My mindset heading into today's practice:

☐ Calm
☐ Focused
☐ Tired
☐ Pumped
☐ Nervous
☐ Something else: _____

If I had to rate my mood out of 10: _____

AFTER PRACTICE

One thing that went well:

_____

_____

One thing I would do differently next time:

_____

_____

Today I had the most fun ...

_____

_____

My mindset after today's practice:

☐ Confident
☐ Frustrated
☐ Proud
☐ Unfocused
☐ Strong
☐ Something else: _____

One word to describe today's practice:

_____

If I had to rate my mood out of 10: _____

Today's Date:_____

BEFORE PRACTICE

Today I am most excited about:

_____

_____

One thing I feel nervous or unsure about:

_____

_____

My focus today is:

_____

_____

My mindset heading into today's practice:

☐ Calm
☐ Focused
☐ Tired
☐ Pumped
☐ Nervous
☐ Something else: _____

If I had to rate my mood out of 10: _____

AFTER PRACTICE

One thing that went well:

_____

_____

One thing I would do differently next time:

_____

_____

Today I had the most fun ...

_____

_____

My mindset after today's practice:

☐ Confident
☐ Frustrated
☐ Proud
☐ Unfocused
☐ Strong
☐ Something else: _____

One word to describe today's practice:

_____

If I had to rate my mood out of 10: _____

Today's Date:_____

BEFORE PRACTICE

Today I am most excited about:

_____

_____

One thing I feel nervous or unsure about:

_____

_____

My focus today is:

_____

_____

My mindset heading into today's practice:

☐ Calm
☐ Focused
☐ Tired
☐ Pumped
☐ Nervous
☐ Something else: _____

If I had to rate my mood out of 10: _____

AFTER PRACTICE

One thing that went well:

_____

_____

One thing I would do differently next time:

_____

_____

Today I had the most fun ...

_____

_____

My mindset after today's practice:

☐ Confident
☐ Frustrated
☐ Proud
☐ Unfocused
☐ Strong
☐ Something else: _____

One word to describe today's practice:

_____

If I had to rate my mood out of 10: _____

Today's Date:_____

BEFORE PRACTICE

Today I am most excited about:

_____

_____

One thing I feel nervous or unsure about:

_____

_____

My focus today is:

_____

_____

My mindset heading into today's practice:

☐ Calm
☐ Focused
☐ Tired
☐ Pumped
☐ Nervous
☐ Something else: _____

If I had to rate my mood out of 10: _____

AFTER PRACTICE

One thing that went well:

_____

_____

One thing I would do differently next time:

_____

_____

Today I had the most fun ...

_____

_____

My mindset after today's practice:

☐ Confident
☐ Frustrated
☐ Proud
☐ Unfocused
☐ Strong
☐ Something else: _____

One word to describe today's practice:

_____

If I had to rate my mood out of 10: _____

Today's Date:_____

BEFORE PRACTICE

Today I am most excited about:

_____

_____

One thing I feel nervous or unsure about:

_____

_____

My focus today is:

_____

_____

My mindset heading into today's practice:

☐ Calm
☐ Focused
☐ Tired
☐ Pumped
☐ Nervous
☐ Something else: _____

If I had to rate my mood out of 10: _____

AFTER PRACTICE

One thing that went well:

_____

_____

One thing I would do differently next time:

_____

_____

Today I had the most fun ...

_____

_____

My mindset after today's practice:

- ☐ Confident
- ☐ Frustrated
- ☐ Proud
- ☐ Unfocused
- ☐ Strong
- ☐ Something else: _____

One word to describe today's practice:

_____

If I had to rate my mood out of 10: _____

Today's Date:_____

BEFORE PRACTICE

Today I am most excited about:

_____

_____

One thing I feel nervous or unsure about:

_____

_____

My focus today is:

_____

_____

My mindset heading into today's practice:

☐ Calm
☐ Focused
☐ Tired
☐ Pumped
☐ Nervous
☐ Something else: _____

If I had to rate my mood out of 10: _____

AFTER PRACTICE

One thing that went well:

_____

_____

One thing I would do differently next time:

_____

_____

Today I had the most fun ...

_____

_____

My mindset after today's practice:

☐ Confident
☐ Frustrated
☐ Proud
☐ Unfocused
☐ Strong
☐ Something else: _____

One word to describe today's practice:

_____

If I had to rate my mood out of 10: _____

Today's Date:_____

BEFORE PRACTICE

Today I am most excited about:

_____
_____

One thing I feel nervous or unsure about:

_____
_____

My focus today is:

_____
_____

My mindset heading into today's practice:

☐ Calm
☐ Focused
☐ Tired
☐ Pumped
☐ Nervous
☐ Something else: _____

If I had to rate my mood out of 10: _____

AFTER PRACTICE

One thing that went well:

_____

_____

One thing I would do differently next time:

_____

_____

Today I had the most fun ...

_____

_____

My mindset after today's practice:

☐ Confident
☐ Frustrated
☐ Proud
☐ Unfocused
☐ Strong
☐ Something else: _____

One word to describe today's practice:

_____

If I had to rate my mood out of 10: _____

Today's Date:_____

BEFORE PRACTICE

Today I am most excited about:

_____

_____

One thing I feel nervous or unsure about:

_____

_____

My focus today is:

_____

_____

My mindset heading into today's practice:

☐ Calm
☐ Focused
☐ Tired
☐ Pumped
☐ Nervous
☐ Something else: _____

If I had to rate my mood out of 10: _____

AFTER PRACTICE

One thing that went well:

_____

_____

One thing I would do differently next time:

_____

_____

Today I had the most fun ...

_____

_____

My mindset after today's practice:

☐ Confident
☐ Frustrated
☐ Proud
☐ Unfocused
☐ Strong
☐ Something else: _____

One word to describe today's practice:

_____

If I had to rate my mood out of 10: _____

Today's Date:_____

BEFORE PRACTICE

Today I am most excited about:

_____

_____

One thing I feel nervous or unsure about:

_____

_____

My focus today is:

_____

_____

My mindset heading into today's practice:

☐ Calm
☐ Focused
☐ Tired
☐ Pumped
☐ Nervous
☐ Something else: _____

If I had to rate my mood out of 10: _____

AFTER PRACTICE

One thing that went well:

_____

_____

One thing I would do differently next time:

_____

_____

Today I had the most fun ...

_____

_____

My mindset after today's practice:

☐ Confident
☐ Frustrated
☐ Proud
☐ Unfocused
☐ Strong
☐ Something else: _____

One word to describe today's practice:

_____

If I had to rate my mood out of 10: _____

Today's Date:_____

BEFORE PRACTICE

Today I am most excited about:

_____

_____

One thing I feel nervous or unsure about:

_____

_____

My focus today is:

_____

_____

My mindset heading into today's practice:

☐ Calm
☐ Focused
☐ Tired
☐ Pumped
☐ Nervous
☐ Something else: _____

If I had to rate my mood out of 10: _____

AFTER PRACTICE

One thing that went well:

_____

_____

One thing I would do differently next time:

_____

_____

Today I had the most fun ...

_____

_____

My mindset after today's practice:

☐ Confident
☐ Frustrated
☐ Proud
☐ Unfocused
☐ Strong
☐ Something else: _____

One word to describe today's practice:

_____

If I had to rate my mood out of 10: _____

Today's Date:_____

BEFORE PRACTICE

Today I am most excited about:

_____

_____

One thing I feel nervous or unsure about:

_____

_____

My focus today is:

_____

_____

My mindset heading into today's practice:

☐ Calm

☐ Focused

☐ Tired

☐ Pumped

☐ Nervous

☐ Something else: _____

If I had to rate my mood out of 10: _____

AFTER PRACTICE

One thing that went well:

_____

_____

One thing I would do differently next time:

_____

_____

Today I had the most fun ...

_____

_____

My mindset after today's practice:

☐ Confident
☐ Frustrated
☐ Proud
☐ Unfocused
☐ Strong
☐ Something else: _____

One word to describe today's practice:

_____

If I had to rate my mood out of 10: _____

Today's Date:_____

BEFORE PRACTICE

Today I am most excited about:

_____

_____

One thing I feel nervous or unsure about:

_____

_____

My focus today is:

_____

_____

My mindset heading into today's practice:

☐ Calm
☐ Focused
☐ Tired
☐ Pumped
☐ Nervous
☐ Something else: _____

If I had to rate my mood out of 10: _____

AFTER PRACTICE

One thing that went well:

_____

_____

One thing I would do differently next time:

_____

_____

Today I had the most fun ...

_____

_____

My mindset after today's practice:

☐ Confident
☐ Frustrated
☐ Proud
☐ Unfocused
☐ Strong
☐ Something else: _____

One word to describe today's practice:

_____

If I had to rate my mood out of 10: _____

Today's Date:_____

BEFORE PRACTICE

Today I am most excited about:

_____

_____

One thing I feel nervous or unsure about:

_____

_____

My focus today is:

_____

_____

My mindset heading into today's practice:

☐ Calm
☐ Focused
☐ Tired
☐ Pumped
☐ Nervous
☐ Something else: _____

If I had to rate my mood out of 10: _____

AFTER PRACTICE

One thing that went well:

_____

_____

One thing I would do differently next time:

_____

_____

Today I had the most fun ...

_____

_____

My mindset after today's practice:

☐ Confident
☐ Frustrated
☐ Proud
☐ Unfocused
☐ Strong
☐ Something else: _____

One word to describe today's practice:

_____

If I had to rate my mood out of 10: _____

Today's Date:_____

BEFORE PRACTICE

Today I am most excited about:

_____

_____

One thing I feel nervous or unsure about:

_____

_____

My focus today is:

_____

_____

My mindset heading into today's practice:

☐ Calm
☐ Focused
☐ Tired
☐ Pumped
☐ Nervous
☐ Something else: _____

If I had to rate my mood out of 10: _____

AFTER PRACTICE

One thing that went well:

_____

_____

One thing I would do differently next time:

_____

_____

Today I had the most fun ...

_____

_____

My mindset after today's practice:

☐ Confident
☐ Frustrated
☐ Proud
☐ Unfocused
☐ Strong
☐ Something else: _____

One word to describe today's practice:

_____

If I had to rate my mood out of 10: _____

Today's Date:_____

BEFORE PRACTICE

Today I am most excited about:

_____

_____

One thing I feel nervous or unsure about:

_____

_____

My focus today is:

_____

_____

My mindset heading into today's practice:

☐ Calm

☐ Focused

☐ Tired

☐ Pumped

☐ Nervous

☐ Something else: _____

If I had to rate my mood out of 10: _____

AFTER PRACTICE

One thing that went well:

_____

_____

One thing I would do differently next time:

_____

_____

Today I had the most fun ...

_____

_____

My mindset after today's practice:

☐ Confident
☐ Frustrated
☐ Proud
☐ Unfocused
☐ Strong
☐ Something else: _____

One word to describe today's practice:

_____

If I had to rate my mood out of 10: _____

Today's Date:_____

BEFORE PRACTICE

Today I am most excited about:

_____

_____

One thing I feel nervous or unsure about:

_____

_____

My focus today is:

_____

_____

My mindset heading into today's practice:

☐ Calm
☐ Focused
☐ Tired
☐ Pumped
☐ Nervous
☐ Something else: _____

If I had to rate my mood out of 10: _____

AFTER PRACTICE

One thing that went well:

_____

_____

One thing I would do differently next time:

_____

_____

Today I had the most fun ...

_____

_____

My mindset after today's practice:

☐ Confident
☐ Frustrated
☐ Proud
☐ Unfocused
☐ Strong
☐ Something else: _____

One word to describe today's practice:

_____

If I had to rate my mood out of 10: _____

Today's Date:_____

BEFORE PRACTICE

Today I am most excited about:

_____

_____

One thing I feel nervous or unsure about:

_____

_____

My focus today is:

_____

_____

My mindset heading into today's practice:

☐ Calm
☐ Focused
☐ Tired
☐ Pumped
☐ Nervous
☐ Something else: _____

If I had to rate my mood out of 10: _____

AFTER PRACTICE

One thing that went well:

_____

_____

One thing I would do differently next time:

_____

_____

Today I had the most fun ...

_____

_____

My mindset after today's practice:

☐ Confident
☐ Frustrated
☐ Proud
☐ Unfocused
☐ Strong
☐ Something else: _____

One word to describe today's practice:

_____

If I had to rate my mood out of 10: _____

Today's Date:_____

BEFORE PRACTICE

Today I am most excited about:

_____

_____

One thing I feel nervous or unsure about:

_____

_____

My focus today is:

_____

_____

My mindset heading into today's practice:

☐ Calm
☐ Focused
☐ Tired
☐ Pumped
☐ Nervous
☐ Something else: _____

If I had to rate my mood out of 10: _____

AFTER PRACTICE

One thing that went well:

_____

_____

One thing I would do differently next time:

_____

_____

Today I had the most fun ...

_____

_____

My mindset after today's practice:

☐ Confident
☐ Frustrated
☐ Proud
☐ Unfocused
☐ Strong
☐ Something else: _____

One word to describe today's practice:

_____

If I had to rate my mood out of 10: _____

Today's Date:_____

BEFORE PRACTICE

Today I am most excited about:

_____

_____

One thing I feel nervous or unsure about:

_____

_____

My focus today is:

_____

_____

My mindset heading into today's practice:

☐ Calm
☐ Focused
☐ Tired
☐ Pumped
☐ Nervous
☐ Something else: _____

If I had to rate my mood out of 10: _____

AFTER PRACTICE

One thing that went well:

_____

_____

One thing I would do differently next time:

_____

_____

Today I had the most fun ...

_____

_____

My mindset after today's practice:

☐ Confident
☐ Frustrated
☐ Proud
☐ Unfocused
☐ Strong
☐ Something else: _____

One word to describe today's practice:

_____

If I had to rate my mood out of 10: _____

Today's Date:_____

BEFORE PRACTICE

Today I am most excited about:

_____

_____

One thing I feel nervous or unsure about:

_____

_____

My focus today is:

_____

_____

My mindset heading into today's practice:

☐ Calm
☐ Focused
☐ Tired
☐ Pumped
☐ Nervous
☐ Something else: _____

If I had to rate my mood out of 10: _____

AFTER PRACTICE

One thing that went well:

_____

_____

One thing I would do differently next time:

_____

_____

Today I had the most fun ...

_____

_____

My mindset after today's practice:

☐ Confident
☐ Frustrated
☐ Proud
☐ Unfocused
☐ Strong
☐ Something else: _____

One word to describe today's practice:

_____

If I had to rate my mood out of 10: _____

Today's Date:_____

BEFORE PRACTICE

Today I am most excited about:

_____

_____

One thing I feel nervous or unsure about:

_____

_____

My focus today is:

_____

_____

My mindset heading into today's practice:

☐ Calm

☐ Focused

☐ Tired

☐ Pumped

☐ Nervous

☐ Something else: _____

If I had to rate my mood out of 10: _____

AFTER PRACTICE

One thing that went well:

_____

_____

One thing I would do differently next time:

_____

_____

Today I had the most fun ...

_____

_____

My mindset after today's practice:

☐ Confident
☐ Frustrated
☐ Proud
☐ Unfocused
☐ Strong
☐ Something else: _____

One word to describe today's practice:

_____

If I had to rate my mood out of 10: _____

Today's Date:_____

BEFORE PRACTICE

Today I am most excited about:

_____

_____

One thing I feel nervous or unsure about:

_____

_____

My focus today is:

_____

_____

My mindset heading into today's practice:

☐ Calm
☐ Focused
☐ Tired
☐ Pumped
☐ Nervous
☐ Something else: _____

If I had to rate my mood out of 10: _____

AFTER PRACTICE

One thing that went well:

_____

_____

One thing I would do differently next time:

_____

_____

Today I had the most fun ...

_____

_____

My mindset after today's practice:

☐ Confident
☐ Frustrated
☐ Proud
☐ Unfocused
☐ Strong
☐ Something else: _____

One word to describe today's practice:

_____

If I had to rate my mood out of 10: _____

Today's Date:_____

BEFORE PRACTICE

Today I am most excited about:

_____

_____

One thing I feel nervous or unsure about:

_____

_____

My focus today is:

_____

_____

My mindset heading into today's practice:

☐ Calm
☐ Focused
☐ Tired
☐ Pumped
☐ Nervous
☐ Something else: _____

If I had to rate my mood out of 10: _____

AFTER PRACTICE

One thing that went well:

_____

_____

One thing I would do differently next time:

_____

_____

Today I had the most fun ...

_____

_____

My mindset after today's practice:

☐ Confident
☐ Frustrated
☐ Proud
☐ Unfocused
☐ Strong
☐ Something else: _____

One word to describe today's practice:

_____

If I had to rate my mood out of 10: _____

Today's Date:_____

BEFORE PRACTICE

Today I am most excited about:

_____

_____

One thing I feel nervous or unsure about:

_____

_____

My focus today is:

_____

_____

My mindset heading into today's practice:

☐ Calm
☐ Focused
☐ Tired
☐ Pumped
☐ Nervous
☐ Something else: _____

If I had to rate my mood out of 10: _____

AFTER PRACTICE

One thing that went well:

_____

_____

One thing I would do differently next time:

_____

_____

Today I had the most fun ...

_____

_____

My mindset after today's practice:

☐ Confident
☐ Frustrated
☐ Proud
☐ Unfocused
☐ Strong
☐ Something else: _____

One word to describe today's practice:

_____

If I had to rate my mood out of 10: _____

Today's Date:_____

BEFORE PRACTICE

Today I am most excited about:

_____

_____

One thing I feel nervous or unsure about:

_____

_____

My focus today is:

_____

_____

My mindset heading into today's practice:

☐ Calm
☐ Focused
☐ Tired
☐ Pumped
☐ Nervous
☐ Something else: _____

If I had to rate my mood out of 10: _____

AFTER PRACTICE

One thing that went well:

_____

_____

One thing I would do differently next time:

_____

_____

Today I had the most fun ...

_____

_____

My mindset after today's practice:

☐ Confident
☐ Frustrated
☐ Proud
☐ Unfocused
☐ Strong
☐ Something else: _____

One word to describe today's practice:

_____

If I had to rate my mood out of 10: _____

Today's Date:_____

BEFORE PRACTICE

Today I am most excited about:

_____

_____

One thing I feel nervous or unsure about:

_____

_____

My focus today is:

_____

_____

My mindset heading into today's practice:

☐ Calm
☐ Focused
☐ Tired
☐ Pumped
☐ Nervous
☐ Something else: _____

If I had to rate my mood out of 10: _____

AFTER PRACTICE

One thing that went well:

_____

_____

One thing I would do differently next time:

_____

_____

Today I had the most fun ...

_____

_____

My mindset after today's practice:

☐ Confident
☐ Frustrated
☐ Proud
☐ Unfocused
☐ Strong
☐ Something else: _____

One word to describe today's practice:

_____

If I had to rate my mood out of 10: _____

Today's Date:_____

BEFORE PRACTICE

Today I am most excited about:

_____

_____

One thing I feel nervous or unsure about:

_____

_____

My focus today is:

_____

_____

My mindset heading into today's practice:

☐ Calm

☐ Focused

☐ Tired

☐ Pumped

☐ Nervous

☐ Something else: _____

If I had to rate my mood out of 10: _____

AFTER PRACTICE

One thing that went well:

_____

_____

One thing I would do differently next time:

_____

_____

Today I had the most fun ...

_____

_____

My mindset after today's practice:

☐ Confident
☐ Frustrated
☐ Proud
☐ Unfocused
☐ Strong
☐ Something else: _____

One word to describe today's practice:

_____

If I had to rate my mood out of 10: _____

Today's Date:_____

BEFORE PRACTICE

Today I am most excited about:

_____

_____

One thing I feel nervous or unsure about:

_____

_____

My focus today is:

_____

_____

My mindset heading into today's practice:

☐ Calm
☐ Focused
☐ Tired
☐ Pumped
☐ Nervous
☐ Something else: _____

If I had to rate my mood out of 10: _____

AFTER PRACTICE

One thing that went well:

_____

_____

One thing I would do differently next time:

_____

_____

Today I had the most fun ...

_____

_____

My mindset after today's practice:

☐ Confident
☐ Frustrated
☐ Proud
☐ Unfocused
☐ Strong
☐ Something else: _____

One word to describe today's practice:

_____

If I had to rate my mood out of 10: _____

Today's Date:_____

BEFORE PRACTICE

Today I am most excited about:

_____

_____

One thing I feel nervous or unsure about:

_____

_____

My focus today is:

_____

_____

My mindset heading into today's practice:

☐ Calm
☐ Focused
☐ Tired
☐ Pumped
☐ Nervous
☐ Something else: _____

If I had to rate my mood out of 10: _____

AFTER PRACTICE

One thing that went well:

_____

_____

One thing I would do differently next time:

_____

_____

Today I had the most fun ...

_____

_____

My mindset after today's practice:

☐ Confident
☐ Frustrated
☐ Proud
☐ Unfocused
☐ Strong
☐ Something else: _____

One word to describe today's practice:

_____

If I had to rate my mood out of 10: _____

Today's Date:_____

BEFORE PRACTICE

Today I am most excited about:

_____

_____

One thing I feel nervous or unsure about:

_____

_____

My focus today is:

_____

_____

My mindset heading into today's practice:

☐ Calm
☐ Focused
☐ Tired
☐ Pumped
☐ Nervous
☐ Something else: _____

If I had to rate my mood out of 10: _____

AFTER PRACTICE

One thing that went well:

_____

_____

One thing I would do differently next time:

_____

_____

Today I had the most fun ...

_____

_____

My mindset after today's practice:

☐ Confident
☐ Frustrated
☐ Proud
☐ Unfocused
☐ Strong
☐ Something else: _____

One word to describe today's practice:

_____

If I had to rate my mood out of 10: _____

Today's Date:_____

BEFORE PRACTICE

Today I am most excited about:

_____

_____

One thing I feel nervous or unsure about:

_____

_____

My focus today is:

_____

_____

My mindset heading into today's practice:

☐ Calm
☐ Focused
☐ Tired
☐ Pumped
☐ Nervous
☐ Something else: _____

If I had to rate my mood out of 10: _____

AFTER PRACTICE

One thing that went well:

_____

_____

One thing I would do differently next time:

_____

_____

Today I had the most fun ...

_____

_____

My mindset after today's practice:

☐ Confident
☐ Frustrated
☐ Proud
☐ Unfocused
☐ Strong
☐ Something else: _____

One word to describe today's practice:

_____

If I had to rate my mood out of 10: _____

Today's Date:_____

BEFORE PRACTICE

Today I am most excited about:

_____

_____

One thing I feel nervous or unsure about:

_____

_____

My focus today is:

_____

_____

My mindset heading into today's practice:

☐ Calm
☐ Focused
☐ Tired
☐ Pumped
☐ Nervous
☐ Something else: _____

If I had to rate my mood out of 10: _____

AFTER PRACTICE

One thing that went well:

_____

_____

One thing I would do differently next time:

_____

_____

Today I had the most fun ...

_____

_____

My mindset after today's practice:

☐ Confident
☐ Frustrated
☐ Proud
☐ Unfocused
☐ Strong
☐ Something else: _____

One word to describe today's practice:

_____

If I had to rate my mood out of 10: _____

Today's Date:_____

BEFORE PRACTICE

Today I am most excited about:

_____

_____

One thing I feel nervous or unsure about:

_____

_____

My focus today is:

_____

_____

My mindset heading into today's practice:

☐ Calm

☐ Focused

☐ Tired

☐ Pumped

☐ Nervous

☐ Something else: _____

If I had to rate my mood out of 10: _____

AFTER PRACTICE

One thing that went well:

_____

_____

One thing I would do differently next time:

_____

_____

Today I had the most fun ...

_____

_____

My mindset after today's practice:

☐ Confident
☐ Frustrated
☐ Proud
☐ Unfocused
☐ Strong
☐ Something else: _____

One word to describe today's practice:

_____

If I had to rate my mood out of 10: _____

Today's Date:_____

BEFORE PRACTICE

Today I am most excited about:

_____

_____

One thing I feel nervous or unsure about:

_____

_____

My focus today is:

_____

_____

My mindset heading into today's practice:

☐ Calm
☐ Focused
☐ Tired
☐ Pumped
☐ Nervous
☐ Something else: _____

If I had to rate my mood out of 10: _____

AFTER PRACTICE

One thing that went well:

_____

_____

One thing I would do differently next time:

_____

_____

Today I had the most fun ...

_____

_____

My mindset after today's practice:

☐ Confident
☐ Frustrated
☐ Proud
☐ Unfocused
☐ Strong
☐ Something else: _____

One word to describe today's practice:

_____

If I had to rate my mood out of 10: _____

Today's Date:_____

BEFORE PRACTICE

Today I am most excited about:

_____

_____

One thing I feel nervous or unsure about:

_____

_____

My focus today is:

_____

_____

My mindset heading into today's practice:

☐ Calm
☐ Focused
☐ Tired
☐ Pumped
☐ Nervous
☐ Something else: _____

If I had to rate my mood out of 10: _____

AFTER PRACTICE

One thing that went well:

_____

_____

One thing I would do differently next time:

_____

_____

Today I had the most fun ...

_____

_____

My mindset after today's practice:

☐ Confident
☐ Frustrated
☐ Proud
☐ Unfocused
☐ Strong
☐ Something else: _____

One word to describe today's practice:

_____

If I had to rate my mood out of 10: _____

Today's Date:_____

BEFORE PRACTICE

Today I am most excited about:

_____

_____

One thing I feel nervous or unsure about:

_____

_____

My focus today is:

_____

_____

My mindset heading into today's practice:

☐ Calm

☐ Focused

☐ Tired

☐ Pumped

☐ Nervous

☐ Something else: _____

If I had to rate my mood out of 10: _____

AFTER PRACTICE

One thing that went well:

_____

_____

One thing I would do differently next time:

_____

_____

Today I had the most fun ...

_____

_____

My mindset after today's practice:

☐ Confident
☐ Frustrated
☐ Proud
☐ Unfocused
☐ Strong
☐ Something else: _____

One word to describe today's practice:

_____

If I had to rate my mood out of 10: _____

Today's Date:_____

BEFORE PRACTICE

Today I am most excited about:

_____

_____

One thing I feel nervous or unsure about:

_____

_____

My focus today is:

_____

_____

My mindset heading into today's practice:

☐ Calm

☐ Focused

☐ Tired

☐ Pumped

☐ Nervous

☐ Something else: _____

If I had to rate my mood out of 10: _____

AFTER PRACTICE

One thing that went well:

_____

_____

One thing I would do differently next time:

_____

_____

Today I had the most fun ...

_____

_____

My mindset after today's practice:

☐ Confident
☐ Frustrated
☐ Proud
☐ Unfocused
☐ Strong
☐ Something else: _____

One word to describe today's practice:

_____

If I had to rate my mood out of 10: _____

Today's Date:_____

BEFORE PRACTICE

Today I am most excited about:

_____

_____

One thing I feel nervous or unsure about:

_____

_____

My focus today is:

_____

_____

My mindset heading into today's practice:

☐ Calm
☐ Focused
☐ Tired
☐ Pumped
☐ Nervous
☐ Something else: _____

If I had to rate my mood out of 10: _____

AFTER PRACTICE

One thing that went well:

_____

_____

One thing I would do differently next time:

_____

_____

Today I had the most fun ...

_____

_____

My mindset after today's practice:

☐ Confident
☐ Frustrated
☐ Proud
☐ Unfocused
☐ Strong
☐ Something else: _____

One word to describe today's practice:

_____

If I had to rate my mood out of 10: _____

Today's Date:_____

BEFORE PRACTICE

Today I am most excited about:

_____

_____

One thing I feel nervous or unsure about:

_____

_____

My focus today is:

_____

_____

My mindset heading into today's practice:

- [ ] Calm
- [ ] Focused
- [ ] Tired
- [ ] Pumped
- [ ] Nervous
- [ ] Something else: _____

If I had to rate my mood out of 10: _____

AFTER PRACTICE

One thing that went well:

_____

_____

One thing I would do differently next time:

_____

_____

Today I had the most fun ...

_____

_____

My mindset after today's practice:

☐ Confident
☐ Frustrated
☐ Proud
☐ Unfocused
☐ Strong
☐ Something else: _____

One word to describe today's practice:

_____

If I had to rate my mood out of 10: _____

Today's Date:_____

BEFORE PRACTICE

Today I am most excited about:

_____

_____

One thing I feel nervous or unsure about:

_____

_____

My focus today is:

_____

_____

My mindset heading into today's practice:

☐ Calm
☐ Focused
☐ Tired
☐ Pumped
☐ Nervous
☐ Something else: _____

If I had to rate my mood out of 10: _____

AFTER PRACTICE

One thing that went well:

_____

_____

One thing I would do differently next time:

_____

_____

Today I had the most fun ...

_____

_____

My mindset after today's practice:

☐ Confident
☐ Frustrated
☐ Proud
☐ Unfocused
☐ Strong
☐ Something else: _____

One word to describe today's practice:

_____

If I had to rate my mood out of 10: _____

Today's Date:_____

BEFORE PRACTICE

Today I am most excited about:

_____

_____

One thing I feel nervous or unsure about:

_____

_____

My focus today is:

_____

_____

My mindset heading into today's practice:

☐ Calm
☐ Focused
☐ Tired
☐ Pumped
☐ Nervous
☐ Something else: _____

If I had to rate my mood out of 10: _____

AFTER PRACTICE

One thing that went well:

_____

_____

One thing I would do differently next time:

_____

_____

Today I had the most fun ...

_____

_____

My mindset after today's practice:

☐ Confident
☐ Frustrated
☐ Proud
☐ Unfocused
☐ Strong
☐ Something else: _____

One word to describe today's practice:

_____

If I had to rate my mood out of 10: _____

Today's Date:_____

BEFORE PRACTICE

Today I am most excited about:

_____

_____

One thing I feel nervous or unsure about:

_____

_____

My focus today is:

_____

_____

My mindset heading into today's practice:

☐ Calm
☐ Focused
☐ Tired
☐ Pumped
☐ Nervous
☐ Something else: _____

If I had to rate my mood out of 10: _____

AFTER PRACTICE

One thing that went well:

_____

_____

One thing I would do differently next time:

_____

_____

Today I had the most fun ...

_____

_____

My mindset after today's practice:

☐ Confident
☐ Frustrated
☐ Proud
☐ Unfocused
☐ Strong
☐ Something else: _____

One word to describe today's practice:

_____

If I had to rate my mood out of 10: _____

Today's Date:_____

BEFORE PRACTICE

Today I am most excited about:

_____

_____

One thing I feel nervous or unsure about:

_____

_____

My focus today is:

_____

_____

My mindset heading into today's practice:

☐ Calm
☐ Focused
☐ Tired
☐ Pumped
☐ Nervous
☐ Something else: _____

If I had to rate my mood out of 10: _____

AFTER PRACTICE

One thing that went well:

_____

_____

One thing I would do differently next time:

_____

_____

Today I had the most fun ...

_____

_____

My mindset after today's practice:

☐ Confident
☐ Frustrated
☐ Proud
☐ Unfocused
☐ Strong
☐ Something else: _____

One word to describe today's practice:

_____

If I had to rate my mood out of 10: _____

Unstoppable
/ˌən-ˈstä-pə-bəl/adj
: incapable of being stopped
I'm so powerful
I don't need batteries to play
I'm confident
I'm focused
I'm resilient
Yeah, I'm unstoppable today

You're almost out of pages! You can use this QR code to head over to Strong Girl Publishing to order your next journal.

StrongGirlPublishing.com/unstoppable

Today's Date:_____

BEFORE PRACTICE

Today I am most excited about:

_____

_____

One thing I feel nervous or unsure about:

_____

_____

My focus today is:

_____

_____

My mindset heading into today's practice:

☐ Calm
☐ Focused
☐ Tired
☐ Pumped
☐ Nervous
☐ Something else: _____

If I had to rate my mood out of 10: _____

AFTER PRACTICE

One thing that went well:

_____

_____

One thing I would do differently next time:

_____

_____

Today I had the most fun ...

_____

_____

My mindset after today's practice:

☐ Confident
☐ Frustrated
☐ Proud
☐ Unfocused
☐ Strong
☐ Something else: _____

One word to describe today's practice:

_____

If I had to rate my mood out of 10: _____

Today's Date:_____

BEFORE PRACTICE

Today I am most excited about:

_____

_____

One thing I feeling nervous or unsure about:

_____

_____

My focus today is:

_____

_____

My mindset heading into today's practice:

☐ Calm
☐ Focused
☐ Tired
☐ Pumped
☐ Nervous
☐ Something else: _____

If I had to rate my mood out of 10: _____

AFTER PRACTICE

One thing that went well:

_____

_____

One thing I would do differently next time:

_____

_____

Today I had the most fun ...

_____

_____

My mindset after today's practice:

☐ Confident
☐ Frustrated
☐ Proud
☐ Unfocused
☐ Strong
☐ Something else: _____

One word to describe today's practice:

_____

If I had to rate my mood out of 10: _____

Today's Date:_____

BEFORE PRACTICE

Today I am most excited about:

_____

_____

One thing I feel nervous or unsure of about:

_____

_____

My focus today is:

_____

_____

My mindset heading into today's practice:

☐ Calm
☐ Focused
☐ Tired
☐ Pumped
☐ Nervous
☐ Something else: _____

If I had to rate my mood out of 10: _____

AFTER PRACTICE

One thing that went well:

_____

_____

One thing I would do differently next time:

_____

_____

Today I had the most fun ...

_____

_____

My mindset after today's practice:

☐ Confident
☐ Frustrated
☐ Proud
☐ Unfocused
☐ Strong
☐ Something else: _____

One word to describe today's practice:

_____

If I had to rate my mood out of 10: _____

You are unstoppable. Not because you do not have failures and doubts. But because you continue on despite them.

UNSTOPPABLE

Step 3:
Competitions

 PACKING FOR COMPETITION

Being unstoppable starts before you even hit the field, track, or court. Packing your bag the right way helps you feel ready, focused, and confident.

This is to help you remember what you need—and avoid those "oops I forgot my uniform" kind of days.

Not all weather is created equally. There are a few weather scenarios below, plus a blank one for weather we have not thought of! You can always come back to add forgotten items.

Take some time here and jot down a few notes about any packing issues you've had in the past. What have you forgotten often? Is there any piece of gear you wish you always had in your bag? What's the wildest weather you've ever practiced in?

_____

_____

_____

_____

_____

_____

_____

Need to make more lists? There are additional 'Packing for Competition' sheets at stronggirlpublishing.com/unstoppable.

Once you're packed for competition, tag us on Instagram - @yellow_running_shoes and @stronggirlpublishing - to share with us what your competition bag looks like!

 HOT & ☀ SUNNY DAYS

Uniform/race kit: _____

_____

_____

Equipment: _____

_____

For Warm-up: _____

_____

For After: _____

_____

Pre-competition snacks: _____

During-competition snacks: _____

Post-competition snacks: _____

☐ Sunscreen   ☐ Extra-large water bottle

My sport specific extras: _____

_____

_____

 RAINY DAYS

Uniform/race kit: _____

_____

_____

Equipment: _____

_____

For Warm-up: _____

_____

For After: _____

_____

Pre-competition snacks: _____

During-competition snacks: _____

Post-competition snacks: _____

☐ Rain Coat & Umbrella   ☐ Plastic Bag

My sport specific extras: _____

_____

_____

❄ COLD & ❄ WINDY DAYS

Uniform/race kit: _____

_____

_____

Equipment: _____

_____

For Warm-up: _____

_____

For After: _____

_____

Pre-competition snacks: _____

During-competition snacks: _____

Post-competition snacks: _____

☐ Extra Coat   ☐ Towel or Blanket

My sport specific extras: _____

_____

_____

OTHER WEATHER: _____

Uniform/race kit: _____

_____

_____

Equipment: _____

_____

For Warm-up: _____

_____

For After Practice: _____

_____

Pre-competition snacks: _____

During-competition snacks: _____

Post-competition snacks: _____

☐ _____ ☐ _____

My sport specific extras: _____

_____

_____

STEP 3: COMPETITIONS

These pages will guide you through everything you need to think about the before your event to help you feel **Unstoppable**.

Because competition days can feel big. There's excitement, nerves, questions, and adrenaline. Whether it's a local meet or a big tournament, this section is here to help you feel prepared, calm, and confident—in both your body and your brain.

You've put in the work. You've trained your body. You've trained your mindset. You've been practicing how to be unstoppable—one practice at a time. Now it's time to bring that same energy, focus, and belief into competition.

You'll plan for:

✈️ Travel
- Where is the competition?
- What time do I need to leave?
- Do I need snacks, a playlist, or something to help me stay calm?

👕 Clothing & Uniform
- What do I need to wear to compete?
- Do I need warm-ups or layers for before/after?
- What gear or equipment do I need?

🌤️ Weather
- What's the forecast?
- Do I need sunscreen? Rain gear? Layers?

🌐 Mindset & Mantra
- What's one thing I want to remind myself going into this event?
- (Examples: "Trust my training." "Stay calm and breathe." "I belong here." "**I am unstoppable.**")

🍎 Food & Fuel
- What am I eating the night before?
- What am I eating the morning of?
- Do I need snacks or drinks for during or after?

💤 Rest & Recovery
- What time do I need to go to bed the night before?
- How can I help myself get good sleep?
- What's my wind-down routine?

Date of Competition: _____

BEFORE COMPETITION

Name of event/meet/game: _____

Where is it happening: _____

Start time of the event/meet/game: _____

What time do I need to arrive: _____

What time do I need to start warming up : _____

When do I need to leave home: _____

Snacks & Fuel

The night before, my pre-competition meal is:

_____

Pre-competition snacks: _____

During-competition snacks: _____

Post-competition snacks: _____

☐ Extra-large water bottle   ☐ Sports Drink

BEFORE COMPETITION

How do I want to feel today?

☐ Confident   ☐ Strong
☐ Calm   ☐ Focused
☐ Brave   ☐ Grateful
☐ Something else: _____

My Mantra for today (Something short that pumps you up or keeps you steady):

_____

_____

One thing I want to focus on today:

_____

_____

One thing I will let go of today:

_____

_____

I'm reminding myself, I'm **Unstoppable** because:

_____

_____

AFTER COMPETITION

One thing that went well competing today:

_____

_____

One thing I would do differently next time:

_____

_____

Today I had the most fun ...

_____

_____

My mindset after today's competition:

☐ Confident
☐ Frustrated
☐ Proud
☐ Unfocused
☐ Strong
☐ Something else: _____

One word to describe today's competition:

_____

If I had to rate my mood out of 10: _____

Date of Competition: _____

BEFORE COMPETITION

Name of event/meet/game: _____

Where is it happening: _____

Start time of the event/meet/game: _____

What time do I need to arrive: _____

What time do I need to start warming up : _____

When do I need to leave home: _____

Snacks & Fuel

The night before, my pre-competition meal is:

_____

Pre-competition snacks: _____

During-competition snacks: _____

Post-competition snacks: _____

☐ Extra-large water bottle ☐ Sports Drink

BEFORE COMPETITION

How do I want to feel today?

☐ Confident   ☐ Strong
☐ Calm   ☐ Focused
☐ Brave   ☐ Grateful
☐ Something else: _____

My Mantra for today (Something short that pumps you up or keeps you steady):

_____

_____

One thing I want to focus on today:

_____

_____

One thing I will let go of today:

_____

_____

I'm reminding myself, I'm **Unstoppable** because:

_____

_____

AFTER COMPETITION

One thing that went well competing today:

_____

_____

One thing I would do differently next time:

_____

_____

Today I had the most fun …

_____

_____

My mindset after today's competition:

☐ Confident
☐ Frustrated
☐ Proud
☐ Unfocused
☐ Strong
☐ Something else: _____

One word to describe today's competition:

_____

If I had to rate my mood out of 10: _____

Date of Competition: _____

BEFORE COMPETITION

Name of event/meet/game: _____

Where is it happening: _____

Start time of the event/meet/game: _____

What time do I need to arrive: _____

What time do I need to start warming up : _____

When do I need to leave home: _____

Snacks & Fuel

The night before, my pre-competition meal is:

_____

Pre-competition snacks: _____

During-competition snacks: _____

Post-competition snacks: _____

☐ Extra-large water bottle ☐ Sports Drink

BEFORE COMPETITION

How do I want to feel today?

☐ Confident ☐ Strong
☐ Calm ☐ Focused
☐ Brave ☐ Grateful
☐ Something else: _____

My Mantra for today (Something short that pumps
you up or keeps you steady):

_____

_____

One thing I want to focus on today:

_____

_____

One thing I will let go of today:

_____

_____

I'm reminding myself, I'm **Unstoppable** because:

_____

_____

AFTER COMPETITION

One thing that went well competing today:

_____

_____

One thing I would do differently next time:

_____

_____

Today I had the most fun ...

_____

_____

My mindset after today's competition:

☐ Confident
☐ Frustrated
☐ Proud
☐ Unfocused
☐ Strong
☐ Something else: _____

One word to describe today's competition:

_____

If I had to rate my mood out of 10: _____

Date of Competition: _____

BEFORE COMPETITION

Name of event/meet/game: _____

Where is it happening: _____

Start time of the event/meet/game: _____

What time do I need to arrive: _____

What time do I need to start warming up : _____

When do I need to leave home: _____

Snacks & Fuel

The night before, my pre-competition meal is:

_____

Pre-competition snacks: _____

During-competition snacks: _____

Post-competition snacks: _____

☐ Extra-large water bottle ☐ Sports Drink

BEFORE COMPETITION

How do I want to feel today?

- [ ] Confident
- [ ] Calm
- [ ] Brave
- [ ] Something else: _____

- [ ] Strong
- [ ] Focused
- [ ] Grateful

My Mantra for today (Something short that pumps you up or keeps you steady):

_____

_____

One thing I want to focus on today:

_____

_____

One thing I will let go of today:

_____

_____

I'm reminding myself, I'm **Unstoppable** because:

_____

_____

AFTER COMPETITION

One thing that went well competing today:

_____

_____

One thing I would do differently next time:

_____

_____

Today I had the most fun ...

_____

_____

My mindset after today's competition:

☐ Confident
☐ Frustrated
☐ Proud
☐ Unfocused
☐ Strong
☐ Something else: _____

One word to describe today's competition:

_____

If I had to rate my mood out of 10: _____

Date of Competition: _____

BEFORE COMPETITION

Name of event/meet/game: _____

Where is it happening: _____

Start time of the event/meet/game: _____

What time do I need to arrive: _____

What time do I need to start warming up : _____

When do I need to leave home: _____

Snacks & Fuel

The night before, my pre-competition meal is:

_____

Pre-competition snacks: _____

During-competition snacks: _____

Post-competition snacks: _____

☐ Extra-large water bottle ☐ Sports Drink

BEFORE COMPETITION

How do I want to feel today?

☐ Confident   ☐ Strong
☐ Calm   ☐ Focused
☐ Brave   ☐ Grateful
☐ Something else: _____

My Mantra for today (Something short that pumps you up or keeps you steady):

_____

_____

One thing I want to focus on today:

_____

_____

One thing I will let go of today:

_____

_____

I'm reminding myself, I'm **Unstoppable** because:

_____

_____

AFTER COMPETITION

One thing that went well competing today:

_____

_____

One thing I would do differently next time:

_____

_____

Today I had the most fun ...

_____

_____

My mindset after today's competition:

☐ Confident
☐ Frustrated
☐ Proud
☐ Unfocused
☐ Strong
☐ Something else: _____

One word to describe today's competition:

_____

If I had to rate my mood out of 10: _____

You are....

UNSTOPPABLE
UNSTOPPABLE
UNSTOPPABLE
UNSTOPPABLE
UNSTOPPABLE
UNSTOPPABLE
UNSTOPPABLE
UNSTOPPABLE
UNSTOPPABLE
UNSTOPPABLE
UNSTOPPABLE
UNSTOPPABLE

This work is grounded in evidence and research. Some of the research informing this work includes:

Coaching Association of Canada. (2022). Mental Health in Sport. Ottawa: Coaching Association of Canada.

Costa, A. L. (2000). Habits of Mind. The Institute for Habits of Mind.

Durand-Bush, N., Joseph, B., van den Berg, F., Richard, V., & Bloom, G. A. (2022). The Gold Medal Profile for Sport Psychology (GMP-SP),. Journal of Applied Sport Psychology, https://doi.org/10.1080/10413200.2022.2055224.

International Olympic Committee. (n.d.). IOC Mental Health in Elite Athletes Toolkit. Retrieved from Athlete 365: https://olympics.com/athlete365/mentally-fit/mentallyfit-toolkit-resources/

Magness, S. (2022). Do Hard Things: Why We Get Resilience Wrong and the Surprising Science of Real Toughness. New York: HarperOne.

Van Slingerland, K. (2020). Review of the Literature: Coach & Athlete Wellbeing. (self-published).

Vernacchia, R. A. (2003). Inner Strength: The Mental Dynamics of Athletic Performance. Palo Alto: Warde Publishers.

Dr. Sasha Gollish has been dreaming of writing this book since completing the Coaching Association of Canada's Advanced Coaching Diploma in 2015. **Unstoppable** is rooted in the final project she developed during that program—one focused on helping athletes build confidence, reflect meaningfully, and strengthen their mental performance from the inside out, to help them have more best days.

Sasha is a Team Canada middle- and long-distance runner, a Pan Am Games medalist, and a lifelong learner of what it means to grow through sport and challenge. She's also a coach, an engineer with a PhD in engineering, a proud stepmom, a speaker, and a passionate leader working to create more inclusive, supportive environments in sport and beyond. She's the co-founder of Yellow Running Shoes, a research-driven, athlete-focused initiative dedicated to bridging the gap between sport science, mental health, and real-world application. She believes that every athlete—no matter their age, ability, experience, or result—deserves tools to feel seen, to feel strong, and to feel unstoppable.

www.ingramcontent.com/pod-product-compliance
Lightning Source LLC
Chambersburg PA
CBHW051207120626
46547CB00013B/1240